Poetics

In Plain and Simple English

BOOKCAPS

BookCaps™ Study Guides
www.bookcaps.com

© 2012. All Rights Reserved.

Table of Contents

ABOUT THIS SERIES 4

I 5

II 8

III 10

IV 12

V 15

VI 17

VII 22

VII 24

IX 25

X 29

XI 30

XII 32

XIII 33

XIV 36

XV 39

XVI 42

XVII 45

XVIII	47
XIX	50
XX	51
XXI	54
XXII	58
XXIII	63
XXIV	66
XXV	70
XXVI	76

About This Series

The "Classic Retold" series started as a way of telling classics for the modern reader—being careful to preserve the themes and integrity of the original. Whether you want to understand Shakespeare a little more or are trying to get a better grasp of the Greek classics, there is a book waiting for you!

The series is expanding every month. Visit BookCaps.com to see all the books in the series, and while you are there join the Facebook page, so you are first to know when a new book comes out.

I

I plan to write of poetry as a whole and of the various types of poetry, discussing the main features of each type. I shall examine how the plot has to be structured to create a good poem; the number of parts which make up a poem and their nature; I shall also examine anything else which comes into the scope of the same inquiry. Let us follow the natural order and begin with first principles.

Epic, Tragic, Comic and Dithyrambic (hymns sung at festivals in honor of Dionoysus) poetry, and most types of music played on the flute and the lyre, are all born from types of imitation (i.e. recreating emotion and action). However, they are different in three ways: the medium, the voice or instruments used and the manner of the imitation; these are all unique in each case.

For just as there are some people who, deliberately or through force of habit, copy and represent various things through the use of colour and shape, or with their voices, so in all the arts mentioned above the imitation is produced through rhythm, language or harmony; these things may be used singly or mixed together.

So in the music of the flute and the lyre, only harmony and rhythm are used. This is the same in other, essentially similar, arts, such as the playing of the shepherd's pipe. In dancing, only rhythm is used. Even dancing represents character, emotion and action through rhythmical movement.

There is another art which imitates, in either prose or verse (if in verse it can use different meters or just one), by only using language, but it has not been given a name up to now. There is no common term which could be used to describe the mimes of Sophron and Xenarchus, and the Socratic dialogues, on the one hand, and on the other poetry in iambic, elegiac or similar meters. People do add the word "maker" or "poet" to the name of the meter and speak of elegiac poets or epic poets (that is, ones writing in hexameter), as if it is not the emotion which makes the poet, simply the type of rhythm they are using. Even when a medical or scientific work is brought out in verse then it is customary to call the author a poet, yet Homer and Empedocoles have nothing in common but their use of meter; one is a poet, the other is a physicist. Even if a poet were to combine all different kinds of meter in his poetry, as Chaeremon did in "Centaur", we should still give him the general name of "poet."

Then again there are some arts which use all the means mentioned above, rhythm, music and meter. These include Dithyrambic and Nomic (sung at religious festivals) poetry, and also Comedy and Tragedy; the difference between them is that in the first type all three are used together, whereas in Comedy and Tragedy first one means is used and then another.

These, then, are the differences between the arts with respect to the imitation of reality.

II

Since the things being imitated are men in action, and these men must be of either a high or low type (for these divisions are mainly a matter of moral character, which can de distinguished by being good or bad), it follows that men must be represented as being better than they really are, worse, or the same. The same happens in painting. Polygnotus showed men as more noble than they are, Pauson showed them as less noble, and Dionysius drew them as they are.

Now it is clear that each type of imitation mentioned above will have these differences, and imitating things they will each become a unique genre. Differences can be found even in things such as dancing, flute playing and playing the lyre. The same is true with words, whether it is prose or verse unaccompanied by music. For example, Homer makes men better than they are; Clepohon portrays them as they are; Hegemon the Thasian, the creator of parodies, and Nicochares, the author of the Deiliad, makes them worse than they are. The same is true in the two types of religious songs mentioned; different types may be shown within these, just as Timotheus and Philoxenus showed the Cyclops in different ways. These differences also distinguish between Tragedy and Comedy: Comedy aims to show men as worse than they are in real life, Tragedy to show them as better.

III

There is a third difference: the way in which each thing may be represented. Even when the medium is the same, and dealing with the same subject, the poet may imitate by using a narrator (in which case he can take on the voice of another personality, as Homer does, or speak directly in his own voice) or by showing us all his characters as living and moving in front of us.

So as we said at the beginning, these are the three different things which go to establish what category an artistic imitation fits into; the medium, the subjects, and the manner. From one point of view, as they both imitate higher types of character, Sophocles is the same kind of imitator as Homer; from another point of view Sophocles is of the same kind as Aristophanes, for they both use people acting in their imitations. This is why, some people say, the word "drama" can be given to poems when they represent action. For the same reason the Dorians claim to have invented both Comedy and Tragedy. The Megarians also claim to have invented Comedy; not only those in Greece, who say it originated under their democracy, but also the Megarians of Sicily, for the comic poet Epicharmus, who is much earlier than Chionides and Magnes, came from there. Some Dorians in the Peloponnese also claim to have invented Comedy. They offer linguistic examples to back up their claims. They say that villages outside their cities are called, in their language, "komai" (the Athenians call them "domai"); they say the name does not come from "komazein" ("to revel") but because, as they were excluded from the city, the comedians wandered from village to village ("kata komas"). They also point out that the Dorian word for "doing" is "dran" while the Athenian is "prattein".

This has said enough about the number and features of different types of imitation.

IV

Poetry in general seems to come from two causes, both of which are ingrained in human nature. The first is that man seems to be born with an instinct for imitation, far more than any other creature, and the first way he learns is through imitation. The second, and equally important, cause is that all humans take pleasure in seeing things imitated. Experience shows us that this is true. Things which in themselves cause us pain or disgust give us great pleasure when accurately reproduced, for example low animals and dead bodies. The reason for this is that learning causes great pleasure, not just for philosophers but for men in general (whose capacity for learning is, however, more limited). So men enjoy seeing a likeness because they may find themselves learning or deducing things from it, perhaps in identifying the individual represented. If you have not seen the original then the pleasure comes from the skill in the making, the coloring or some other cause, not from the accuracy of the imitation.

Imitation, then, is part of human nature. Another part is an instinct for harmony and rhythm (meter in poetry is obviously rhythmic). Early men began with a natural gift for rhythm which they refined until their crude improvisations became Poetry.

Poetry then split into two different types, according to the individual character of the writers. The more serious ones imitated noble actions and the deeds of good men. The more trivial ones imitated the actions of people of a lower type, composing satires, while the other type wrote hymns to the gods and works praising famous men. There are no satirical poems which can be dated as being any earlier than Homer, though there probably were many satirical writers before his time. But from Homer onwards there are many examples of satirical poetry: his own "Margites", for example, and other similar works. At this time an appropriate meter for comedy was introduced; so the meter is still called the iambic ("lampooning") measure, being the one people used to lampoon each other. So the early poets were divided into writers of heroic or lampooning verse.

Homer is the greatest poet in the serious style, as he was the only one who combined the dramatic form with excellence of imitation. He also laid down the foundations of comedy, by dramatizing the ridiculous instead of writing personal satire. His comic mock epic Margites is as important to comedy as the Iliad and Odyssey are to tragedy. But when Tragedy and Comedy were developed, each poet followed their natural instincts: the lampooners wrote Comedy and the Epic poets were followed by Tragedians, as drama is a larger and higher form of art.

Whether Tragedy has reached perfection in its forms yet, and whether it should be judged on its own or in relation to its audience, is another question.

Whatever the answer, Tragedy (and Comedy also) was at first simply improvisation. Tragedy was developed by the authors of hymns, while Comedy was developed by the authors of the smutty songs one can still hear in our cities. Tragedy developed in slow steps; as each new element appeared it led to others. It passed through many changes, then it found its natural form and stopped.

Aeschylus was the first to introduce a second actor into drama; he made the chorus less important and gave the main part of the play to speeches. Sophocles raised the number of actors to three, and added settings. It was not until quite recently that the basic plot gave way to one of greater complexity, and the ugly speech of the earlier satires was replaced by the dignified manner of Tragedy. The troachic tertrameter, which was originally used when the poetry was of the Satryic type and was closer to dancing, was replaced by the iambic measure. Once dialogue had been introduced the appropriate meter came naturally. For the iambic measure is, of all measures, the most familiar. This can be seen in the fact that everyday speech most often turns into iambic lines, more than any other type; it rarely turns into hexameters, and only when we speak more formally. The additions to the number of "episodes" (acts), and the other additions which we learn of from tradition, must be taken as read; to discuss them in detail would be a large project.

V

Comedy is, as we have said, an imitation of characters of the lowest type. However they are not what one would call bad, their ridiculousness being simply a type of ugliness. The characters have some flaw or ugliness which is not painful or destructive. An obvious example is the comic mask, which is ugly and distorted but does not look like a person in pain.

The changes through which Tragedy developed, and the writers who introduced them, are well known, whereas Comedy has no history, because it was not taken seriously in its early days. It was a long time before the magistrates in charge of the drama allowed a poet to have a comic chorus; until then the performers were volunteers. Comedy was already an established form by the time the first recognised comic poets are heard of. It is not known who invented the masks, prologues or increased the number of actors. As for the plot, it originally came from Sicily, but of the Athenian writers if was Crates who was the first to abandon the iambic or lampooning meter and establish set themes and plots.

Epic poetry and Tragedy are similar in that they are both imitations of characters of a higher type. The difference between them is that Epic poetry only allows one type of meter and is narrative in form. They also are different in their length; the action of a Tragedy takes place, as nearly as possible, within a single day, whereas the Epic has no time limits. This is now the second point of difference although at first Tragedy and Epic poetry shared the same freedom with regard to time.

Of the parts which go to make up these two types, some are shared by both and some are unique to tragedy, so that a person who knows what is good or bad Tragedy will also know about Epic poetry. All the elements of an Epic poem are found in Tragedy, but not all the elements of Tragedy are found in an Epic poem.

VI

We will speak later of poetry which uses hexameter verse, and of Comedy. Let us now discuss Tragedy, continuing to define it formally, developing what has already been said.

Tragedy, then, is an imitation of action that is serious, complete and has a certain grandeur. Its language is decorated with each kind of different artistic form, different kinds being found in different parts of the play. It takes the form of action, not narrative. It uses pity and fear to achieve catharsis (the removal of emotions by feeling them through seeing them portrayed). By "decorated" with reference to language I mean language which has rhythm, harmony and song. By "different kinds in different parts" I mean that some parts of the play are given in verse alone, while others are given in song. As tragic imitation means that people will be acting it follows that props will be part of the Tragedy. Next we must consider Song and Diction, for these are the medium of the artwork. By "Diction" I simply mean the arrangement of the words in metrical patterns; as for "Song" it is a term whose use everyone understands.

Tragedy is the imitation of real life, and that implies the involvement of individual people, who will of course have individual qualities of both character and thought. We define actions by the character and thought involved in them, and all actions spring from character and thought. Whether the drama succeeds or fails depends on the action. So the Plot is the imitation of action, for by plot here I mean the arrangement of the incidents. By Character I mean certain attributes which we give to individual people in the drama. Thought is required whenever a statement is made or when a general truth is spoken. Every Tragedy, therefore, must have six parts, and these parts will determine its quality. The parts are Plot, Character, Diction, Thought, Spectacle (visual elements) and Song. Two of the parts are concerned with the type of artwork, one with its manner, and three with the things being imitated. We may say that these elements have been used by every single poet. In fact, every play contains Spectacular elements as well as Character, Plot, Diction, Song and Thought.

The most important thing of all is the structure of the incidents. For Tragedy is not an imitation of men but of action and life. Life is made up of actions and death is a type of action, not a quality. Character determines the quality of a man, but it is their actions which make them happy or otherwise. Dramatic action, therefore, is not aimed at representing character; character is secondary to the action. So incidents and the plot are the purpose of Tragedy, and the purpose is the main thing. One cannot have a Tragedy without action, but one can have one without character. The tragedies of most of our modern poets fail in their representation of character, and this is true of poets in general. It is the same in painting, and this is the difference between Zeuxis and Polygnotus. Polygnotus is good at showing character: Zeuxis' style has no ethical quality. So if you put together a set of speeches which show character, nicely written with respect to diction and thought, you will not achieve the desired effect of Tragedy nearly so well as a play which, however much it lacks those qualities, has a plot and well devised incidents. It can also be said that the most powerful elements of emotional interest in Tragedy – Peripeteia (reversal of the situation) and Recognition scenes – are parts of the plot. Another proof of the importance of the plot is that novice playwrights always reach perfection in diction and character depiction before they learn how to construct a plot. This was the case with almost all the early poets.

Plot then is the first principle and as it were the soul of a tragedy: Character is second. The same thing can be seen in painting. The most beautiful colors, thrown on unskilfully, will not give as much pleasure as a simple chalk sketch. So Tragedy is the imitation of an action, and all its parts are mainly concerned with this.

In third place is Thought, that is saying what is possible and relevant in a given situation. In the case of speech, this is the function of Political art and the art of rhetoric. This can be seen by the fact that the earlier poets make their characters speak like politicians; our current poets use the language of rhetoric. Character shows the moral purpose of a man and what he will choose or avoid. Therefore speeches which do not make this clear, or in which the speaker does not choose or avoid anything in any way, do not show character. Thought, on the other hand, is shown when something is proved or disproved, or a general truth is spoken.

Fourth in the elements of Tragedy is Diction. This means, as I have already said, the expression of meaning through words. This is essentially the same in both verse and prose.

Of the remaining elements Song has the most important place as a decoration.

The visual Spectacle does have an emotional attraction of its own but of all the parts it is the least artistic and least connected with the art of poetry. For it is certain that the power of Tragedy can be felt independently of the staging and the actors. Besides, the production of the Spectacle depends more on the art of the set designer than the art of the poet.

VII

Having established these principles, let us now discuss how a plot should be structured, since this is the first and most important thing in tragedy.

Now, according to our definition, Tragedy is an imitation of an action that is complete, whole, and of a certain size (for something can be complete but lacking size). To be complete there must be a beginning, a middle and end. A beginning does not follow anything else, but it is the thing from which other things follow. An end, on the other hand, is a thing which follows on from others, either naturally, or due to a rule, but has nothing following it. A middle follows on from something and has something following on from it. A well constructed plot, therefore, does not begin or end at random but follows these principles.

Again, a beautiful object, whether it is a living thing or any object made up of parts, must not only have its parts arranged in an orderly manner but must be of a certain size. So a very small creature cannot be beautiful, for it cannot be properly appreciated, being seen in the blink of an eye. Nor, again, can something enormous be beautiful, as the eye cannot appreciate all its parts at once, so there is no sense of unity and completeness for the spectator. This would be the case, for example, if something were a thousand miles long. Just as in the case of living things a certain size is necessary which can be seen all at once, so in the plot a certain length is necessary, and it must be a length which the memory can cope with. Length which is limited for the purposes of dramatic competition or attractive presentation has no place in artistic theory. For if it was the rule that a hundred tragedies had to be in a competition together, their lengths would have to be set by a stopwatch, as we have been told was in fact the case in past times. But there is a limit to length set by the nature of drama itself, which is this: the longer a piece is, the more beautiful that length will make it, provided that the whole thing is clearly presented. To define the proper length roughly, we may say that it should be able to allow the sequence of events, according to the laws of probability and necessity, to allow bad fortune to turn to good, or vice versa.

VII

Consistency of plot does not, as some people think, necessitate a straightforward hero. There are many emotional incidents in a man's life and they cannot be reduced to a single entity, similarly we cannot take all the actions of a man and condense them to a single action. This is the error, it seems, made by all poets who have written a Heraclid (work about Hercules), a Theseid (work about Theseus) or other poems of that type. They imagine that as Hercules was one man, then his story must be a single entity. But Homer, the best in this as in everything else – whether from skill or natural genius – seems to have happily hit on the right method. When he composed the Odyssey he did not include all the adventures of Odysseus such as his wound on Parnassus, or his feigned madness at the gathering of the army, incidents between which there was no obvious connection. What he did was to make the Odyssey, and also the Iliad, center round an action that is, in our sense of the word, singular. So, as for example when a painter paints a portrait he paints the whole person, the plot, being an imitation of an action, must make all the action a complete whole. The different parts should be joined so that if any one were moved or removed altogether the whole thing would be wrong. Anything which makes no discernible difference, whether it is present or absent, is not an organic part of the whole and so is not necessary.

IX

It can also be seen from what has been said that the function of the poet is not to describe what has happened but what may happen: what is possible according to the laws of nature and probability. The difference between the poet and the historian is not a matter of just writing in verse or prose. The work of Herodotus might be turned into a poem and it would still be history, with meter no less than it was without. The real difference is that the historian tells what has happened, the poet what may happen. Poetry, therefore, is more philosophical than history, for poetry deals with universal themes and history with one particular person or event. By universal I mean exploring how a person of a certain type will react in speech or action to a certain event, according to the laws of nature and chance, and it is this universality the poet aims for with his characters, the one representing a whole. The particular is, for example, what Alcibades did or suffered. In Comedy this can be seen, as the poet builds his plot on the lines of probability, and then gives generic names to his characters – unlike the lampooners who write about particular individuals. But tragedians still use real names, in order to make their writing about what is possible seem believable. If something has not happened we do not straight away feel that it could have happened; but if the drama is about something that has happened then it is believable as it is a fact. Still, there are even some tragedies in which there are only one or two famous real names, with the rest being invented. In others there are no well-known names, such as Agathon's Antheus, where the incidents and names are both fictional, and yet they still give us pleasure. We must not, therefore, rigidly stick to existing legends, which are the usual subjects for Tragedy. Indeed, it would be absurd to try. Only a few people know the legends these dramas are based on, but when they are performed all enjoy them. It therefore follows that the poet or "creator" should create plots rather than verses, because he is a poet because he imitates, and what he imitates are actions, and actions make plots. Even if he does choose an historical subject, he is still a poet; there is no reason why something that has happened should not conform to the laws of probability and possibility, and if they have that quality within them then he is their creator, or poet.

Of all types of plots and actions, the episodic are the worst. I call a plot "episodic" if the episodes or acts follow each other in an improbable or unnatural sequence. Bad poets write pieces like these because they are bad poets; good poets write them to please their actors, for as they write pieces to be shown in competition they stretch the plot too far and break up its natural continuity.

Tragedy is not only an imitation of complete action, but also of events which inspire fear or pity. This effect works best when such events come on us by surprise, and is even better if, at the same time, they follow the law of cause and effect. The tragic feeling will then be greater than if they happened as "one-offs" or by accident – even coincidences are most effective when they seem to be inevitable. An example is the statue of Mitys at Argos, which fell upon his murderer when he (the murderer) was watching a festival and killed him. Events like this do not seem to be pure chance. Therefore plots which are constructed on these principles are the best.

X

Plots are either Simple or Complex, for real life, on which plots are based, obviously can be simple or complex itself. If, in an action, which is singular and continuous as described above, a change of fortune occurs without Reversal of Situation or Recognition, I call it Simple.

A Complex action is one which takes place with such a Reversal, by Recognition, or both. These things should come out of the internal structure of the plot, so that what happens next should seem natural or plausible given what had happened previously. It makes all the difference whether something happens directly due to a past event, or just because it comes next in time.

XI

Reversal of the Situation is a change in which the action switches round to its opposite, as long as it still obeys our rule of probability or naturalness. So in Oedipus, the messenger comes to cheer Oedipus and free him from his concern that he will marry his mother, but by revealing who he is he has the opposite effect. Again in the story of Lynceus, Lynceus is being led away to his death, and Danaus goes with him, meaning to kill him, but because of what has already happened Danaus is killed and Lynceus is saved. Recognition, as the name implies, is a change from ignorance to knowledge, and this produces love or hate between people the poet has marked down for good or bad fortune. The best form of Recognition is when it combines with a Reversal of Situation, as in the Oedipus. There are other forms of recognition, indeed petty inanimate things may in a sense be objects of recognition. We may also recognise whether a person has or has not done some particular action. But the recognition which is most closely connected with the plot and action is, as we have said, the recognition of a person for who they really are. This recognition, combined with reversal, will produce either pity or fear, and by our definition actions producing these effects are the essence of Tragedy. Furthermore such situations determine whether a person will have good or bad fortune. Recognition being between two people , it may be that only one person is recognised by the other – when the second person is already known – or it may be necessary for the recognition to take place on both sides. So Iphegenia is recognised by Orestes by the sending of the letter, but another act of recognition is required for Iphegenia to recognise Orestes.

Two parts, then, of the Plot – Reversal of the Situation and Recognition – depend upon surprises. A third part is the Scene of Suffering. The Scene of Suffering is a destructive or painful action, such as death on the stage, physical agony, wounds and so on.

XII

The parts of the Tragedy which must be treated as elements of the whole have already been mentioned. Now we come to the parts to do with meter and the separate parts into which tragedy is divided, these being Prologue, Episode, Exode and Chroic song, the last of these being divided into Parode and Stasimon. These parts are common to all plays: only some also have songs sung from the stage by actors or the Chorus.

The Prologue is the whole of the tragedy up to the Parode of the Chorus. The Episode is the whole section between the songs of the Chorus. The Exode is the whole of the section which is not followed by a song of the Chorus. Of the Choric parts the Parode is the first uninterrupted speech or song of the Chorus: the Stasimon is a part for the Chorus without anapaests or trochaic terameters: in the Commos the actors and the Chorus join together in a lament. The parts of the tragedy which must be treated as elements of the whole have already been mentioned; now we have listed the parts concerning the meter and the separate parts into which it is divided.

XIII

Following on from what has already been said, we must consider what the poet should aim at, and what he should avoid, when constructing his plots, and how the specific effect of Tragedy is produced.

As detailed previously, a perfect tragedy should be complex, not simple. It should be based on actions which create fear and pity in the audience, as this is the unique feature of tragedy. It is obvious that the change of fortune in the play must not concern a good man whose life moves from riches to hardship; this does not inspire pity or fear, only shock. Nor should it concern a bad man moving from hardship to prosperity, as this is completely against the spirit of Tragedy and has no tragic quality; it does not inspire fear and pity, and it does not please the moral sense. Nor, again, should the downfall of an utter villain be shown. This kind of plot would obviously be morally satisfying, but it would not create either pity or fear. Pity is created by witnessing the downfall of a man through underserved bad luck, and fear is caused by the man being somewhat like ourselves. So seeing a bad man succeed would be neither pitiful nor terrible. So there remains the character between these two extremes, a man who is not perfectly good and just, but whose misfortune is not a result of vice and depravity but some error or frailty. He must be well known and prosperous, a man like Oedipus, Thyestes or other notable men from that type of family.

A well constructed plot should therefore only deal with a single issue, not two as some believe. The change of fortune should not be from bad to good but from good to bad. It should not be the result of vice but of some great error or frailty, and it should happen to a character either such as the one we have described or at least one who leans towards good rather than bad. The way drama has developed confirms this. Initially the poets based their plots on any legend they happened to find. Now the best tragedies are based on the stories of a few families, on the fortunes of Alcmaeon, Oedipus, Oresetes, Meleager, Thyestes, Telephus and those others who have done or suffered something terrible. This is the way a Tragedy should be constructed in order to be perfect. So it is wrong to criticise Euripedes just because he constructs his plays in this manner, with many of them having unhappy endings. These endings are, as we have said, the right ones. The proof of this is that on the stage and in dramatic competitions these plays are the most tragic, and Euripedes, even though he may be criticized with regard to the general management of his subject, is thought of as the most tragic of the poets.

In the second level of tragedies are the type which some people think are the best. Like the Odyssey, these have two plotlines and two different catastrophes for the good and the bad. It is thought to be the best by the audience as it is written for them, with the poet constructing his play according to what the audience wants. This means that the pleasure to be found in these plays is not true tragic pleasure. It is better suited to Comedy, where those who in the play are deadly enemies, like Orestes and Aegisthus, finish the play as friends, and no one is killed.

XIV

Fear and pity may be caused through visual effects, but they may also come from the inner structure of a piece. The latter is the better way and is the mark of the superior poet. The plot should be constructed so that, even without seeing the action on stage, someone who is told the story will thrill with horror and melt with pity on hearing it. This is how we should feel when we hear the story of Oedipus. To produce this effect just through visual effects is less artistic, and relies on external props. Those who attempt to create a Tragedy through the use of props do not create a sense of the terrible but of the monstrous. Such writers do not understand the purpose of Tragedy; they do not know that we should not demand that Tragedy gives us all forms of pleasure, only the ones it is right for it to give. Since the pleasure comes from pity and fear, which is created by imitation, it is obvious that this must be an integral part of the plot.

So we need to examine which circumstances we feel are frightening or pitiful.

Actions which are capable of creating this effect must take place between characters who are either friends, are enemies or do not care about each other. If an enemy kills an enemy we do not feel pity either from the act or the events leading up to it, except inasmuch as the suffering itself can be pitied. The same is true if the two characters involved do not care about each other. But when the tragic incident takes place between those who are near and dear to each other (for example a brother kills, or intends to kill, his brother, a son his father, a mother her son, a son his mother and so on), that is the sort of situation a poet should be looking for. He may not change to plotlines of the established stories – for example, Clytemnestra should still be killed by Orestes, Eriphyle by Alcmaeon – but he ought to show his own creativity and skilful handling of the source material. Let us explain more clearly what is meant by skilful handling.

The action may be done deliberately and with knowledge, as in the work of the earlier poets. For example, Euripedes has Medea killing her children in full knowledge of what she is doing. Alternatively the horrible deed may be done unknowingly, with the perpetrator only discovering afterwards he has killed a friend or a kinsman. The Oedipus of Sophocles is an example of this type. In that play the incident occurs outside the drama on the stage, but there are examples where it happens within the play, such as the Alcmaeon of Astydamas, or Telegonus in the Wounded Odysseus. There is a third type, where a character is about to act, knowing who the victim will be, but then does not. The fourth type is when a character is about to commit an irreversible deed in ignorance, but discovers the facts before it is done. These are the only ways the plot can be made, with the deed either being done or not done, knowingly or unknowingly. Of all these ways, the one where a character is about to act, knowing who the intended victim is, and then does not, is the worst. This type is shocking without being tragic, as there is no disaster. So it is never, or very rarely, found in poetry. There is an example in Antigone, where Haemon threatens to kill Creon. The next, and better way, is that the deed should be done. Even better, it should be done in ignorance, with the truth being discovered afterwards. Then there is nothing to shock us but we are startled by the discovery. The last case is the best, for example as in the Cresphontes when Merope is about to slay her son but recognises who he is and spares his life. Again, in the Helle, the son recognises the mother just as he is about to give her up. This is why the stories of only a few families are suitable for tragedy. For the poets, tragedy came about by happy chance (rather than skill) as they told the tragic stories of these families. So they are forced to only use stories of families whose history contains such tragic incidents.

This is now enough about the structure of action and the right type of plot.

XV

With regard to character there are four things to be aimed at. First, and most important, it must be good. Any speech or action that has a moral purpose will show the speaker's character; if the purpose is good then we know the character is good. This rule applies to all classes. Even a woman can be good, or a slave, even though women can be said to be inferior beings and slaves are quite worthless. The second thing to aim for is suitability. One can show manly courage, but courage in a woman, or cunning intelligence, is not appropriate. Thirdly, a character must be true to life, which is a different thing to goodness and suitability as I have described them here. The fourth thing needed in a character is consistency: although the character may exhibit inconsistency, if he does so he has to always do it, and so be consistent. As an example of pointless bad character we have Menelaus in the Orestes. An example of immodest and inappropriate character is Odysseus' lament in the Scylla, and the speech of Melanippe. Inconsistency is shown in the Iphigenia at Aulis, as Iphigenia the petitioner is nothing like the character we see later.

In the portrayal of character, in the same way as in the structure of the plot, the poet should always aim at what is natural and/or probable. So a person should speak according to their given character, following the laws of nature or probability, in the same way these laws are applied to the way the events follow each other. So it follows that the revealing of the plot, as well as its complexity, must come from the plot itself, not from an artificially introduced element – for example the Medea, or the return of the Greeks in the Iliad. The artificial element should only be used for events outside the drama, for things that happen before or after the timespan of the play which the audience cannot know about and so have to be reported or predicted. Within the action there should be nothing illogical. If it cannot be excluded it should not be an integral part of the tragedy. This is the case with the illogical element of Sophocles' Oedipus.

As Tragedy is the depiction of characters who are higher than the common herd, the example of good portrait painters should be followed. While they reproduce the essential elements of the original they make a likeness which is at the same time accurate but more beautiful than real life. So the poet, when he depicts men who are irritable or lazy, should truly show their character but make them more noble. This is the way Achilles is depicted by Agathon and Homer.

These are the rules which a poet must follow. Also he should not forget to appeal to the senses, which is not essential but naturally happens with poetry, for many mistakes can also be made in this area. But I have written enough about that elsewhere.

XVI

We have already had an explanation of recognition. We will now describe its types.

First we have the least artistic form, which is the most frequently used though a lack of imagination; recognition by signs. Of these signs some are present from birth, such as "the spear which the earth-born race bear on their bodies" or the stars introduced by Carcinus in his Thyestes. Others are signs obtained after birth; some of these are marks on the body, like scars, some are external objects such as necklaces or the little boat in the Tyro through which the discovery is made. Even these types of signs can be handled more or less skilfully. So Odysseus is recognised from his scar in one version by the nurse, in another by the swineherds. The use of objects as proof – and indeed any type of formal proof, with or without objects – is a less artistic type of recognition. A better kind of recognition is one that occurs through an incident, such as the one in the Bath Scene in the Odyssey.

Next on the scale come the recognitions invented by the poet as he likes, and for this reason they lack artistic validity. For example, in the Iphegenia, Orestes reveals his own identity. She makes her identity known through the letter, but he, by simply announcing who he is, is saying what the poet needs, not what the plot needs. This type of recognition is therefore almost as bad as the fault mentioned above:

Orestes might as well have brought objects to prove his identity. Another similar example is the "voice of the shuttle" in Sophocles' Tereus.

The third kind of recognition depends on memory, where the sight of some object wakens a feeling; this happens in Dicaeogenes' Cyprians, where the hero bursts into tears when he sees the picture. Another example is the "Lay of Alcinous", where Odysseus, hearing the minstrel play the lyre, remembers the past and weeps, which shows his recognition.

The fourth kind of recognition comes through the process of reasoning. This happens in the Choephori: "Someone resembling me has come; no one resembles me except Orestes; therefore Orestes has come." The same thing happens with the discovery by Iphigenia in the play of Polyidus the Sophist. It was a natural for Orestes to state, "So I must die at the altar like my sister." So, again, in the Tydeus of Theodectes, the father says, "I came to find my son, and I lose my own life." This happens in the Phineidae: the women, on seeing the place, deduced what their fate would be: "Here we are doomed to die, for here we were cast forth." There is also a composite type of recognition, which involves one of the characters making a wrong deduction, as in the Odysseus Disguised as a Messenger. One character said that nobody else could bend the bow, so Odysseus imagined that the character would recognise the bow which he had not in fact seen. Creating a recognition in this way is a false inference.

But the best of all recognitions are those which come from the plot itself, where the startling discovery is made naturally. This happens in Sophocles' Oedipus, and in the Iphigenia, for it was natural for Iphigenia to want to send a letter. These are the only types of recognition which can do without the artificial help of objects.

XVII

In building the plot and working it out in the proper rhythm, the poet should as far as possible try to imagine the scene before his eyes. In this way, seeing everything as clearly as possible, as if he were in the audience, he will discover what is good in it and be unlikely to overlook any inconsistencies. The need to do this can be seen by the fault in a play by Carcinus. Amphiaraus was on his way from the temple; this fact had escaped the playwright's observation. The piece failed on the stage, as the audience were offended by the oversight.

The poet should also, as much as he can, decide on the appropriate gestures for the actors; those who feel emotion portray it best through natural sympathy with the characters they represent. Someone who is agitated storms, one who is angry rages, in as lifelike a way as possible. So poetry can be thought of either as a happy natural gift or a type of madness. In the first case a man can imitate any character; in the second he becomes something different to himself.

As for the story, whether the poet takes an existing one or creates a new one, he should first sketch out its general outline, then fill in the episodes and the detail. We can see how the general plan should be written by looking at Iphigenis. A young girl is sacrificed – she disappears mysteriously from the sight of those who sacrificed her – she is transported to another country, where the custom is to offer all strangers as a sacrifice to the goddess – she is chosen as a priestess – some time later her brother arrives (the fact that the oracle ordered him to go there for some reason is outside the general plan, as is the purpose of his coming) – he comes, he is seized, and on the point of being sacrificed he reveals who he is. The mode of recognition may be that of Euripedes or of Polydius, in whose play he exclaims very naturally, "So it was not only my sister only, but I too was doomed to be sacrificed." This remark saves him.

After this, with the characters having been given names, it remains to fill in the episodes. It must be ensured that they are relevant to the action. In the case of Orestes, for example, there is the madness which led to his capture and his deliverance due to the rite of purification. In drama, the episodes are short, but they are extended in Epic poetry. We can see that the story of the Odyssey can be stated very briefly: a certain man is absent from home for many years – Posedion follows him jealously and he is wrecked – his home is in a desperate state, with suitors wasting his fortune and plotting against his son – he arrives after a difficult journey – he lets certain people know he is back – he attacks the suitors himself and is saved while he destroys them. That is the plot in a nutshell: everything else is episode.

XVIII

Every tragedy falls into two parts: Complication and Unravelling or Denouement. Incidents which are outside the action are often mixed with the action to form the Complication; then comes the Unravelling. By the Complication I mean everything that happens from the start of the play up until the point when there is the turn towards good or bad fortune. The Unravelling is everything which runs from the turning point until the end. So in the Lynceus of Theodectes the Complication consists of the incidents that are supposed to have happened before the drama and the seizure of the child, and the Unravelling runs from the accusation of murder to the end.

There are four kinds of Tragedy: the Complex, depending entirely on Reversal of Situation and recognition; the Pathetic (where the motive is passion), such as the tragedies concerning Ajax and Ixion; the Ethical (where the motives are ethical), such as the Phthiotides and the Peleus; the fourth kind (we exclude the types which are pure spectacle) is the Simple, exemplified by the Phorcides, the Prometheus and scenes set in Hades. The poet should attempt, if possible, to include all poetic elements; if he cannot manage that he should include as many of the most important elements as possible; this is even more important given the petty critics of modern times. Whereas up to now there have been good poets, each one expert in his own genre, the critics nowadays expect a man to be better than all others in several different areas.

In comparing tragedies and calling them the same or different, the best test is to look at the plot. Plays can be identified as similar where the Complication and the Unravelling are the same. Many poets set up the plot well, but then unfold it badly. Both parts should be mastered equally. The poet should always remember the established rule and not try to make an Epic into a Tragedy – by an Epic I mean one that has many plotlines – as if, for instance, one was to try and make a tragedy out of the entire story of the Iliad. In the Epic poem, because of its length, each part has room to expand to its proper proportions. In the drama the result will be disappointing. The proof is shown by poets who have tried to dramatise the whole story of the Fall of Troy, instead of selecting portions of it, like Euripedes, or have taken the whole story of Niobe, and not a part of her tale, like Aeschylus; these dramas either fail completely or are unpopular when they are staged. Even Agathon has been known to fall into this trap. In his Reversals of the Situation, however, he shows a marvellous skill in his effort to satisfy popular demand – to produce a tragic effect which is satisfying to the moral sense. This effect is produced when the clever rogue, like Sisphyus, is outwitted, or the brave villain is defeated. These things become probable when viewed in Agathon's sense of the word: "it is probable," he says, "that many things will happen which are improbable."

The Chorus should be regarded as one of the actors; it should be an essential part of the whole, and share in the action, in the manner of Sophocles rather than that of Euripedes. With the later poets, their choral songs have so little relevance that they could be fitted into any tragedy. They are just interludes, which is a practice first begun by Agathon. What difference is there between such meaningless choral interludes and moving a speech, or a whole act, from one play to another?

XIX

We still have to discuss Diction and Thought, the other parts of Tragedy having already been discussed. With Thought we may include what is said in the Rhetoric, which is where the subject really belongs. Every effect which has to be produced by speech comes under thought, including proof/disproof, the creation of emotions such as pity, fear, anger etc and the suggestion of importance or triviality. Dramatic incidents share many of these aims, having the objective of creating a sense of fear, pity, importance or plausibility. The only difference is that incidents should be able to make their point without verbal explanation, while the effects in speech are produced by the speaker. What is the point of having a speaker there, if the Thought was revealed in some other way?

Next we must look at Diction. One area which comes under Diction is types of speaking. But this area is part of the art of Delivery and belongs to those who are masters of it. This includes knowing what is a command, a prayer, a statement, a threat, a question, an answer and so on. For a poet to know or not know these things is not vital to his art. Who would accept that Homer is at fault, as Protagoras says he is, when he uses the words, "Sing, goddess, of wrath"? Protagoras says that he seems to be saying a prayer but in fact is giving a command. He says that to tell someone to do something or not do it is a command. This sort of discussion can be omitted here as it belongs to another art, not to poetry.

XX

Language as a whole includes the following parts: Letter, Syllable, Connective, Noun, Verb, Inflexion or Case, Sentence or Phrase.

A Letter is a basic unit of sound which cannot be reduced to its parts, but only one which can form part of a group of sounds, because even animals can make units of sound, none of which I would call a letter. The sound may be a vowel, a semi-vowel, or a mute. A vowel is a sound that can be made without having to use the tongue or lips. A semi-vowel is a sound that is made with the tongue or lips, such as S and R. A mute uses the tongue and lips but does not become audible unless it is added to a vowel sound: examples of this are G and D. They are given their characteristics according to the shape of the mouth and the place within it from which they are produced, whether they are made with an effort of breath or smooth, long or short, high or low pitched or in between. The detail of this area is the province of writers on meter. A Syllable is a meaningless sound, composed of a mute and a vowel: GR without A is a Syllable and is also a Syllable with A: GRA. But the investigation of these differences is also a part of the science of meter.

A Connecting Word is a meaningless sound which neither causes nor stops many sounds coming together to make a meaningful sound. It may come anywhere in a sentence. Or it can be a meaningless sound which can join several meaningful sounds to make another meaningful sound, such as amphi, peri etc. It can be a meaningless sound which marks the beginning, end or division of a sentence, but that cannot stand alone at the beginning of a sentence, such as men, etoi, de etc.

A noun is a composite meaningful sound, which does not indicate passing time, of which no part is itself meaningful, for in double or compound words we do not use each separate part as if it had meaning itself. So in the word "Theodorus", "god-given", we do not give meaning to the separate section "doron" or "gift".

A verb is a composite meaningful sound, which indicates passing time, of which, as with nouns, no part itself has meaning. For "man" or "white" gives no indication of time, but "he walks" or "he has walked" does indicate whether we are in the present or the past.

Inflection can be used with both nouns and verbs, and can be used to show things are related – "of", "to" and so on. It can show whether things are singular or many, as in "man" or "men". It can also change the style and tone of delivery, for example when asking a question or making a command. "Did he go?" and "Go!" are examples of how the same word can be differently inflected.

A Sentence or Phrase is a composite sound which has meaning, and at least some of the parts can have meaning on their own; not every such group of words is made only of verbs and nouns – for example "the definition of man" – but it may omit even the verb. But there will always be some meaningful part, as "in walking" or "Cleon son of Cleon." A sentence or a phrase may be complete in two ways: it can express a single thing, or it can be several parts linked together. So the Iliad is one thing made of many parts linked together, "the definition of man" is a complete thing because its subject is unified.

XXI

There are two kinds of words, simple and double. By simple words I mean those which are made of elements which have no meaning, such as ge, "earth." By double (or compound) I mean those words which are made up of either a meaningful and meaningless element (though when they are placed in a word none of the elements has meaning on its own) or of two elements which are both meaningful. A word may also have three, four or more elements, like so many Massilian expressions, for example "Hermo-caico-xanthus" ("who prayed to father Zeus").

Every word is either current, or strange, or metaphorical, or ornamental, or newly-coined, or lengthened, or contracted, or altered.

By a current or proper word I mean one which is generally used by the people; by strange, a word from another country. The same word can clearly be current for one people and strange for another, but never current and strange for the same people. The word "sigynon" ("lance") is a current term for people from Cyprus but a strange one for us.

Metaphor is the use of a different name by moving the word from a genus to a species, from a species to a genus, between different species or by analogy, that is by comparison. An example of genus to species is, "There lies my ship", because lying at anchor is a subdivision of the word lying. From the smaller to the larger (species to genus) might be, "verily ten thousand noble deeds hath Odysseus wrought,", for ten thousand is a specific large number but here is used o represent the concept of a large number rather than the specific. An example of switching words on the same level is "With blade of bronze drew away the life," and "Cleft the water with the vessel of unyielding bronze." Here "arusai", "to draw away" is used in place of "tamein", "to cleave" and vice versa; both words can mean to take away. Analogy or comparison is when two things have the same relationship as two other things, so we can switch them around and still keep sense. Sometimes we may qualify this by adding the term the moved word was used with in the first place. So the cup is a part of the equipment of Dionysus (god of wine) as the shield is to Ares (god of war). Therefore we may call a cup, "the shield of Dionysus", and a shield, "the cup of Ares." Again, old age has the same relation to life as evening does to day. So evening can be called, "the old age of the day," and old age, "the evening of life," or as Empedocles puts it, "life's setting sun." One can still sometimes use a metaphor even if there is not an interchangeable term available. For example, scattering seed is called sowing, but there is no equivalent word for the way the sun scatters his rays, but still it is the same process. So the poet can create the phrase, "sowing the god-created light." There is another way to use this kind of metaphor. We can apply a different term and then take away one of its usual attributes, so we might call a shield not, "the cup of Ares," but "the wineless cup."

A newly-coined word is one which has never been used anywhere, but is changed for the use of the poet himself. Examples of this type of word are: ernyges, 'sprouters,' for kerata, 'horns'; and areter, 'supplicator', for hiereus, 'priest.'

A word is lengthened when its own vowel is exchanged for a longer one, or when an extra syllable is inserted. A word is contracted when some part of it is removed. Examples of lengthening are: poleos for poleo, Peleiadeo for Peleidou; of contraction: kri, do, and ops, as in mia ginetai amphoteron ops, 'the appearance of both is one.'

An altered word is one in which part of the word keeps its ordinary form, and part is reshaped: such as dexiteron kata mazon, "on the right breast," where dexiteron has been changed to dexion.

Nouns are either masculine, feminine or neuter. Masculine nouns end in N, R, S or some letter joined with S – there are two types of this, PS and X. Feminine nouns end in long vowels; either the vowels which are always long, E and O, or the one that can be lengthened, A. So the number of letters which can end masculine and feminine nouns are the same, as PS and X are the same as the S ending. No nouns naturally end in a silent or short vowel. Only three end in I, meli ("honey"), kommi ("gum") and peperi ("pepper"). There are five nouns ending in U. Neuter nouns end in I,U,N or S.

XXII

The very best style is the one which is clear without being basic. The clearest style is one which only uses current or proper words, but then it is too basic, as in the poetry of Cleophon and Sthenelous. What raises speech above the commonplace is the use of unusual words. By unusual, I mean words which are rare or strange, metaphorical, lengthened: anything which differs from everyday speech. But a style which only uses such words becomes either a riddle or jargon, only comprehensible to experts: if it is solely made up of metaphors it becomes a riddle, if only of unusual words it becomes a jargon. The purpose of a riddle is to state a true fact through an absurd statement. This cannot be done with the use of ordinary words, but it can be done with metaphor. This is the case in the riddle, "A man I saw who on another man had glued the bronze by aid of fire," and other similar ones. A speech that is made up of strange or rare terms is a jargon. It is necessary for style to have a certain amount of these elements, for the strange or rare word, the metaphor and the ornamental word will raise it above the everyday and basic, while the use of proper words will make it understandable. Nothing is better for creating a speech which is clear but far above the everyday than changing words by lengthening, contracting or altering them. By moving away, in exceptional cases, from ordinary speech, the language will become elevated. At the same time, keeping some of the language familiar will allow it to be understood. Those critics who attack these variations in speech and make fun of their authors are wrong. So Eucleides the Elder declared that anyone could be a poet if one were allowed to lengthen syllables as one fancied. He made fun of the practice in his own speech, as in the verse:

"Epicharen eidon Marathonade badizonta,

"I saw Epichares walking to Marathon, "

or,

"ouk an g'eramenos ton ekeinou elleboron.

"Not if you desire his hellebore. "

[N.B. it is impossible to fully render the meaning on the page in English. What Aristotle is quoting is an example where the first sentence is changed into the second through lengthening the words]

To use such techniques in such an obvious way is, of course, ugly and absurd, but all types of poetic writing require moderation. Even metaphors, strange or rare words or similar types of speech would have a similar effect if they were used without care and with the purpose of being ridiculous. We can see how great a difference can be made by using the technique of lengthening in a proper manner by taking Epic poetry and replacing the lengthened words with ordinary ones. If we take a rare or strange word, a metaphor or a similar expression and replace it with a current or proper term then what we are saying will be obvious. For example, Aeschylus and Euripedes both wrote the same iambic line. But Euripides used an unusual term instead of the commonplace one and made his verse seem beautiful and the other one trivial. In Philcoctetes Aeschylus says:

"phagedaina d'he mou sarkas esthiei podos.

"The tumor which is eating the flesh of my foot."

Euripides wrote "feasts on" instead of "feeds on." Again, in the line:

"nun de m'eon oligos te kai outidanos kai aeikes,

we can see a difference if we replace the common words,

"nun de m'eon mikros te kai asthenikos kai aeides.

"Yet a little fellow, weak and ugly."

Or if instead of the line,

"diphron aeikelion katatheis oligen te trapezan,

"Setting an unseemly couch and a meager table,"

we read,

"diphron mochtheron katatheis mikran te trapezan.

"Setting a wretched couch and a puny table."

Or, for eiones booosin, 'the sea shores roar,' eiones krazousin, 'the sea shores screech.'

On the same point, Ariphrades mocked the tragedians for using phrases which would not be found in everyday life, for example domaton apo, "from the house away" instead of apo domaton, "away from the house" ; sethen, ego de nin, "to thee, and I to him"; Achilleos peri, "Achilles about" instead of peri Achilleos, "about Achilles" and so on. He failed to see the point, which is that these phrases elevate the style precisely because they are unusual.

It is most important to use these types of expression correctly, and the same goes for compound words, strange or rare words and so on. But the greatest thing of all is to be able to use metaphor well. This is the one thing that can't be taught; it is the sign of a genius, for it shows that the writer has an eye for resemblances.

Of the various types of word, compound words are best used in dithyrambs, rare words in heroic poetry and metaphors in iambic poetry. In fact in heroic poetry all these types of words can be used. But in iambic verse, which is as close as possible to ordinary speech, the best words are the ones which can be found even in prose. These are the current or proper, the metaphorical and the ornamental.

XXIII

As for the type of poetry which tells a story and only uses one meter, the plot should definitely, as with a tragedy, be constructed according to the principles of drama. It should have as its subjects a single event, whole and complete, and have a beginning, middle and end. This way it will have a completeness like a living organism and give the pleasure it aims for. It will be different to historical writing, which has to present a period of time, not a single action, and show all the things that happened in that period to many different people, however disconnected they are. The sea fight at Salamis and the battle with the Carthiginians in Sicily happened at the same time, but they did not produce a single result: this is the way with events, where one thing may follow another without an end result. This is how, we have to say, most poets structure their work. Again, as has been mentioned before, Homer is head and shoulders above the rest. Even though the Trojan war had a beginning and end he never attempted to cover the whole thing in his poem. It would have been too great a subject and impossible to be taken in at one sitting. If he had tried to keep it to a reasonable length it would have become crowded by the number of events he would have had to fit in. Instead, he took a single part of the war as his plot and allowed in as episodes events from the whole story, such as the catalogue of ships and others, to add interest. All other poets choose a single hero, a single period or a single action, but throw in many parts. This is what happened with the author of the Cypria and Little Iliad. The Iliad and the Odyssey each only have enough material for one tragedy, or at most two, while the Cypria has material for many, and the Little Iliad has material for eight: the Award of the Arms, the Philoctetes, the Neoptolemus, the Eurypylus, the Mendicant Odysseus, the Laconian Women, the Fall of Ilium and the Departure of the Fleet.

XXIV

Epic poetry must have as many types as Tragedy: it must be simple or complex, "ethical" or "pathetic". The parts are also the same, except that Epic poetry does not have songs or stage effects. Like Tragedy, it should have Reversals of the Situation, Recognitions and Scenes of Suffering. Furthermore, the themes and the language should be artistic. In all these areas Homer is our earliest and perfect example. Each of his poems in fact has a double character: the Iliad is both simple and "pathetic" and the Odyssey is complex (for it has many Recognition scenes) and also "ethical". They are also the greatest works in terms of speech and theme.

Epic poetry is different to Tragedy in that it is of a greater length and uses a different meter. We have already described the correct length: the beginning and end should be visible in one go [i.e. it should not be of a length such that the audience cannot grasp the whole story at once]. This condition will be met by writing poems that are shorter than the old epics, of the same length as a group of tragedies presented in a single showing.

Epic poetry, however, can be greatly expanded, for obvious reasons. In Tragedy we cannot have several different plotlines going on at the same time; we can only focus on the stage and what the actors are doing. But the narrative form of Epic poetry allows us to see many events happening at the same time, and as long as they are relevant they add weight and grandeur to the work. The Epic poem has an advantage here which adds to the impressiveness of its effect, in that it can entertain the listener and break up the narrative with different episodes. Too much of the same plot soon bores the audience, and it can make tragedies failures when they are staged.

As for the meter, the heroic meter, the hexameter, has shown itself as the best by standing the test of time. If a narrative poem were now to be written in a different meter, or many meters, it would look odd. Of all meters the heroic is the grandest and weightiest, and so it is most suited to rare words and metaphors; this is another area in which narrative poetry is the best. Conversely, the iambic meter and the trochaic tetrameter are lively rhythms, the first being suitable for action and the second being like dancing. It would be even more ridiculous to mix different meters together, as Chaeremon did. No one has ever composed a great Epic poem in anything other than heroic verse. As we have already said, it is the natural choice.

Homer, who is admirable in all things, is unique in being the only poet who knows what his place in the poem is. The poet should speak as little as possible in his own voice, because when he does then he is not an imitator. Other poets appear all the time in their own work, and imitate others only rarely. Homer, after a brief introduction, straight away brings in a man, a woman or other character; each of them is a well rounded, unique character.

Tragedy requires a certain amount of imaginative events. The unrealistic, on which the imaginative depends, is more easily shown in Epic poetry, because the audience cannot physically see the character. So the pursuit of Hector would be absurd on a stage, with the Greeks having to stand still and Achilles waving them back as if they were moving. But in the Epic poem this absurdity passes unnoticed. The imaginative is pleasing, as we can see from the fact that everyone who tells a story adds something of his own, knowing the listeners will enjoy it. It is Homer who was the main teacher of other poets in the art of skillful lying. The secret lies in a false assumption which people make. Men know that if one thing happens, a second thing may follow from it; so if they see the second thing, they assume that the first must have happened. But this is a wrong inference. So if the first event has not happened, as long as the second event has there is no need to make up the first one; the mind, knowing the second is true, assumes that the first must also have happened. There is an example of this in the Bath Scene of the Odyssey.

So a poet should prefer impossible things which appear logical to possible things which are extremely unlikely. The tragic plot must be logical. Everything illogical should be excluded if possible, and if it cannot be it should at least not be part of the action of the play (for example in Oedipus, when the hero does not know how Laius died); it should not be in the drama, for example in Electra with the messenger's account of the Pythian games, or in the Mysians, when the man comes from Tegea to Mysia and is still speechless. It is no excuse to say such a device has to be there or the plot would be ruined: such a plot should never have been invented. But once the illogical has been introduced and we are told it is real, we have to accept it despite its absurdity. Even in the Odyssey there are irrational incidents, such as when Odysseus is left on the shore of Ithica. Even these might have been intolerable if they were written by a lesser poet, but the skill of the poet allows us to overlook the absurdity.

The writing should be more ornate when there are pauses in the action, when no character or thought is being shown. When they are being shown over elaborate writing actually obscures them.

XXV

We shall now look at the criticisms which writers face, and how to rebut them.

A poet is an imitator, like a painter or any other artist, and so he has to show one of three things: things as they were or are, things how people say or think they are, or things as they should be. Their medium is language, either everyday speech or, if they wish, fine words and metaphors. There are also many changes to the language which we allow the poets to make. To this we should add that accuracy is not as important in poetry as in politics, or in any other art. In poetry there are two types of faults, those which are part of the essence of the poem and those which are incidental. If a poet has chosen to imitate something and has done it incorrectly through a lack of ability, the whole poem is a failure. But if the poet has simply made a mistake, such as showing a horse throwing out both its offside legs at the same time, or made an error concerning medicine or any other art, for example, the error does not fundamentally affect the quality of the poetry. These are the points of view from which we should look at and answer criticism.

Firstly we shall look at matters concerning the poet's own skill. If he describes the impossible, he is guilty of an error, but that error may be justifiable if the artistic purpose is achieved (what this is has already been mentioned) – if this enhances the effect of the poem. The pursuit of Hector is an example of this. If, however, the same purpose could have been achieved as well or better without breaking the rules of poetry then it is not justified. Errors should always be avoided wherever possible.

As before, we must ask if the error is integral to the poetic art, or an external accident. It is worse to represent a hind in a clumsy manner than to now know that it has no horns.

If a critic objects that a description is not true to life, the poet may perhaps answer that it is true to how life ought to be. Sophocles said that he drew men as they ought to be, whilst Euripides showed them as they are. This is a way to answer this criticism. However, there is another way of answering, which is to say that the depiction is how men believe things are; this applies to stories involving the gods. It may be that these stories are as unrealistic as Xenophanes says, neither true to life nor better than life, but they are what men believe. Again, a description might be simply factual and one can defend it on that basis, as in the criticized passage about weapons: "The spears stood upright on their butt-ends"; that was the usual way of standing them then, as it is amongst the Illyrians today.

Again, when we look at whether what someone has said or done is poetically right we must not only look at the act or saying and consider it just in poetic terms. We must ask who said or did it, to whom, how and why; for example, it could be to gain a greater good, or avoid a greater evil.

Other criticisms may be averted if we look closely at the use of language. We may see an unusual word, as in oureas men proton, 'the mules first [he killed],' where the poet actually meant the guards, not mules. Again, Dolon writes, "ill-favored indeed he was to look upon." This does not mean that his body was unshapely but that he had an ugly face, as the Cretans sue the word euides, "well-favored" to mean a handsome face. Again, zoroteron de keraie, "mix the drink livelier", which might be thought to mean make it stronger for a hard drinker in fact means "make it quicker."

Sometimes an expression is metaphorical, as in "Now all gods and men were sleeping through the night", while at the same time we are told, "Often indeed as he turned his gaze to the Trojan plain he marveled at the sound of flutes and pipes." "All" here is a metaphor for "many", as all is a part of many. Also in the verse, "alone she hath no partner" "alone" is metaphorical, meaning as the most famous person she is unique, not that she is literally alone.

The solution to a misunderstanding may lie in the accent or the breathing. So Hippias of Thapos suggested a change in reading so didomen (didomen) de hoi became hou (ou) kataputhetai ombro.

Sometimes the matter may be resolved through use of punctuation, as Empedocles did: 'Of a sudden things became mortal that before had learnt to be immortal, and things unmixed before mixed.'

Or it can be explained through ambiguity of meaning, as in parocheken de pleo nux, where the word pleo could mean more than one thing.

Sometimes it can be explained through the way language has developed: for example any mixed drink is called oinos, "wine". So Ganymede is described as pouring out wine for Zeus, even though the gods do not drink wine. Another example is that ironworkers are called chalkeas, which actually means bronzeworkers. However this example could also be described as a metaphor.

When a word seems to be contradictory, we should consider the ways in which it is intended to be meant in the context of the passage. For example, with Homer's phrase, "there was stayed the spear of bronze" was should ask precisely what was meant by "stopped there." The best way to interpret a passage is to avoid what Glaucon mentions: he says that certain critics leap to unjustified conclusions, and having done so they go on to decide what the work is about based on that conclusion, and criticize a poet for deviating from their assumption if something does not fit with their ideas.

The question about Icarius is an example of this. The critics have decided that he was a Lacedaemonian. Having decided this they think it strange that Telemachus did not meet him when he went to Lacedaemon. But the Cephallenians say that Odysseus took his wife from their people, and that her father was called Icadius, not Icarius. So the whole argument of the critics could be based on a spelling mistake.

In general, when a thing is shown that is impossible it must be justified as being artistically necessary, as showing a higher reality or reflecting general beliefs. With artistic requirements it is better for something to be impossible but likely than for it to be possible but unlikely. It may be true that there were never any men like the ones whom Zeuxis painted. "Yes," we say, "but this impossible thing he has made is better: he was painting the ideal type, which must be better than reality." To justify the illogical we point to the fact that it is commonly believed. We also justify the illogical by pointing out that it does not go against all sense; as said before "It is probable that improbable things will happen."

Things that sound contradictory should be examined by the same rules as are used in debate: we should look at the words to see if he means what he seems to mean. We should answer criticisms by examining what the poet himself says or with reference to what a person of intelligence would assume.

It is right to criticize illogicality, as well as morally bad characters, if they are put in when there is no structural necessity for them. Examples of this practice are the introduction of Aegeus by Euripides and the badness of Menelaus in the Orestes.

So, there are five categories of critical objections. Things are criticized as being impossible, illogical, immoral, inconsistent or unartistic. The criticisms should be answered using the twelve categories detailed above.

XXVI

The question may be asked as to which is the higher artform, Epic or Tragedy. If we think of the less vulgar art as being higher, and this is what always appeals to the better sort of audience, then the art which appeals to everyone is obviously vulgar. The audience is thought to be too dull to understand anything unless the performers throw in something of their own, so they leap about unnecessarily. Bad flute-players dance around to their music, or rush the conductor when they perform the Scylla. It is said that Tragedy has the same fault. We can look at the opinions the older actors had of their successors. Mynniscus used to call Callippides an ape because of his hammy gestures, and Pindarus came in for the same criticism. Tragedy is to Epic what the younger actors were to the older ones. So we are told that Epic poetry is written for a cultivated audience, who don't need gestures, whereas Tragedy is for the general public. Tragedy being vulgar, then, it is clearly the lower of the two.

Now, firstly, this criticism is aimed at the acting, not the poetry, because gestures can just as well be overdone in the reciting of epics, as Sosistratus does, or in song competitions, like Mnasitheus the Opuntian. Secondly, not all gesture should be deplored, any more than all dancing should be, but only those made by bad actors. This was what Callippides was criticized for, and others in our time are criticized for portraying immoral women. But Tragedy, like Epic poetry, can have an effect without any action: it can show its power just by being read. So, if it is superior in every other way, this is not an ingrained fault.

And it is superior, because it has all the elements of the epic – it may even use the same meter – with music and staging added, and these can give great pleasure. It can also be enjoyed just as a text, as well as staged. Furthermore, Tragedy achieves its aims in a shorter timeframe, and this concentration gives more pleasure than an effect which is spread over time and so diluted. Would the Oedipus of Sophocles have the same effect if it was as long as the Iliad? The Epic form is not as perfectly whole as Tragedy: this can be seen from the fact that any Epic poem will provide material for several tragedies. So, if the poet chooses a story which has a perfect unity it will either be too short for an Epic or it will have to be spun out and so lose its power. The length of an Epic must cause some lack of unity if the poem represents several events, like the Iliad and the Odyssey, which have many such parts, each with their own importance. But these poems are as perfect as an Epic can hope to be: they are as close as possible to representing a single action.

If Tragedy, then, is superior to Epic poetry in all these respects, and also is better at achieving its specific artistic aims (for each art should not produce pleasure by chance but the specific pleasure it aims for) then it is clearly the higher art, being better at achieving its aims.

And so we have seen the differences between Tragic and Epic poetry, their types and elements, with the number of each of them and the differences between them. We have seen the reasons a poem can be good or bad, and the objections critics raise and how these may be answered.

Cover Image © lynea - Fotolia.com

Made in the USA
Middletown, DE
20 August 2021